Happy Halloween
Coloring Book

Susan T. Hall

Dover Publications, Inc.
Mineola, New York

Note

It's time to go trick-or-treating, and the cuddly critters on the pages of this book are inviting you along! Join a rabbit magician, pig princess, owl wizard, and more furry friends decked out in all kinds of costumes. Perfect for getting into the Halloween spirit, this book will delight little trick-or-treaters.

A Word From the Artist

I loved coloring books when I was little, and yes, I did stay in between the lines. I thought it was fun to do that, and I still do. The cover of this book is colored with soft leaded colored pencils. You can overlap and make new colors, color softly for light colors and heavy for richer colors. You can use dark colors as shading to add volume to your picture. You can stay inside or go outside of the lines, use whatever colors you like, add patterns, and have fun!

SUSAN T. HALL

Bibliographical Note

Happy Halloween Coloring Book is a new work, first published by Dover Publications, Inc., in 2013.

International Standard Book Number
ISBN-13: 978-0-486-49218-6
ISBN-10: 0-486-49218-4

Manufactured in the United States by LSC Communications
49218406   2018
www.doverpublications.com